ATTACK OF THE KILLER VIDEO BOOK

TIPS AND TRICKS FOR YOUNG DIRECTORS

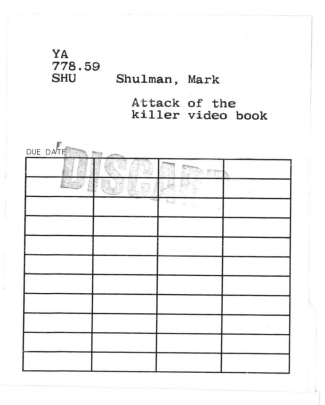

ATTACK OF THE KILLER VIDEO BOOK

TIPS AND TRICKS FOR YOUNG DIRECTORS

BY MARK SHULMAN AND HAZLITT KROG

ART BY MARTHA NEWBIGGING

Annick Press
TORONTO + NEW YORK + VANCOUVER

©2004 Mark Shulman and Hazlitt Krog (text)
©2004 Martha Newbigging (illustrations)
Designed by Sheryl Shapiro

The publisher wishes to thank Colin Foster of Big Woo Films and Philip Hoffman of the York University Department of Film & Video for looking over the manuscript.

Annick Press Ltd.

We acknowledge the support of the Canada Council for the Arts, the Ontario Arts Council, the Government of Ontario through the Ontario Book Publishers Tax Credit program and the Ontario Book Initiative, and the Government of Canada through the Book Publishing Industry Development Program (BPIDP) for our publishing activities.

Cataloging in Publication

Shulman, Mark
        Attack of the killer video book : tips and tricks for young
directors / by Mark Shulman and Hazlitt Krog ; art by Martha Newbigging.

Includes index.
ISBN 1-55037-841-4 (bound).–ISBN 1-55037-840-6 (pbk.)

1. Video recordings–Production and direction–Juvenile literature.
I. Krog, Hazlitt II. Newbigging, Martha III. Title.

PN1992.94.S48 2004   j778.59   C2003-905976-6

The art in this book was hand-drawn, scanned, and then colored in Photoshop.

Distributed in Canada by:	Published in the U.S.A. by Annick Press (U.S.) Ltd.
Firefly Books Ltd.	Distributed in the U.S.A. by:
66 Leek Crescent	Firefly Books (U.S.) Inc.
Richmond Hill, ON	P.O. Box 1338
L4B 1H1	Ellicott Station
	Buffalo, NY 14205

Printed and bound in Belgium.

Visit us at: www.annickpress.com

To my father, who always held the camera
and left us no pictures.
To my daughter, in the hope that you will
someday watch at least some of it.
—M.S.

To my wife Alexia, whose patience,
insight, and love shines a brilliant
light on the future.
—H.K.

To A.T. and M.M., my video art gurus.
—M.N.

ACKNOWLEDGMENTS

For Miriam and Leah Ragen, Andrew and Brendan Finn, and all the other
future visionaries: We want good stories filled with interesting people. Thank
you, thank you, to Hazlitt Krog, for friendship, perseverance, and for sharing
his many talents. Huge thanks to professors Ken Wilson and Joseph DeRoller
of East High School in Rochester, N.Y., for explaining movies so enjoyably.
And thanks to George Eastman, inventor of Kodak film in my hometown.
Without him, we'd all be going to a lot more plays.
    —Mark Shulman

I'd like to acknowledge a few of the many great people who have inspired and
assisted me on my long path to completing this book: Lou CasaBianca, Raúl Essig,
Ned Gorman, Lorna Green and Nicole Moore, Pete Horner and Betty Huang,
Dr. William Jungels, Logan Kelsey, Bob Kovacs, Don Lamoreaux, Barry Levinson,
Andy Lilien, Gina Olmedo, Gregg Olsson, Thornton Prayer, Eric Rewitzer and
Annie Galvin, Diane Samples, John Veltri, and Dzogchen Khenpo Choga
Rinpoche. Special thanks to my co-author, Mark, who has remained a true
friend through thick and thin and especially through rewrites. And a very
special thanks to Dr. Norman and Helen Krog, who gave me more than I'll ever
know, including my start in the real world and then my start in the film world.
    —Hazlitt Krog

GETTING STARTED

Make Fun!

Make Friends!

Make Trouble!

Make a Million Dollars!

Make Videos!

Even if you don't make a million dollars right away, you can make outrageously good videos. All you need is a little creativity, some patience, lots of light, and this book.*

If you want to say something, see something, or save an experience forever, video is the way to go. You can create entertainment or an audiovisual diary. You can practice being a director, writer, actor, singer, or interviewer. And believe it or not, five or ten years later, you'll be happy to see what you looked like at this age. Whatever you choose to do in the age of video, understanding the art and science today can help you take a starring role tomorrow.

You are very wise indeed to be reading this book. We have packed hundreds of tons of useful information and helpful hints into just 64 pages (not including the front and back covers). In fact, by the time you are finished with *this one page*, you will know more than when you began.

For instance, video cameras don't do well when they are dropped. They are not a bath toy. And cameras are more expensive to throw than rocks. See how much you're learning?

The info in this book is a good start. We'll give you the basics, from thinking to planning to shooting to editing, without being scary. And then we'll let you loose on the world. Every videomaker has a story to tell. Just press the REC button, and tell it.

Moves to make before making your movie

Try this simple exercise. Look in the mirror and ask yourself, "Am I a brilliant video master with 'Hollywood Legend' written all over my face?" Now move that face up and down. The answer is "Yes."

*And a video camera.

ROAD MAP

You don't need a lot of money, or experience, or famous friends. Follow this simple route to success.

The Inspiration   10

When video ideas come in a brainstorm, it's customary to shout "Eureka!" (a brand of vacuum cleaner). Some people shout "Hoover!" or "Electrolux!" but it still means you've got a great idea for your video, and that's the first step.

Full Team Ahead   13

Many videos need multiple people. Some are the crew (behind the camera), and others are talent (loosely speaking), and other others sell popcorn on opening night. Some do all three. Don't be a maniac; moviemaking is a team sport. It's more fun to share the details of planning, scripting, shooting, and editing. Let others have input, or they'll leave you holding the camera bag.

The Story   15

Remember screaming about vacuum cleaners? Grab a pen and put that brilliant brainstorm on paper. This helps you keep focused when the craziness of shooting starts, and it gives your team a goal to remember. Don't forget this — there's a quiz later: *Every video tells a story, and everything in the video should help tell the story*. Your video may need a script or a visual storyboard or just a loose set of notes. Without a script, you'll be shooting from the hip and probably miss your target. There are simple tricks to telling a story on video, and learning them will keep your audience coming back for more.

Planning 20

Pre-production is Hollywood lingo for "planning before you get in too deep." First talk with your team and make some decisions about the equipment, costumes, locations, and more. Figure out the *locations* where you're going to shoot. Make a list of the *props* (the parachute, the sword) and *costumes* (the fake nose, the Viking helmet) you're using. Make sure everyone brings what they need – or promised to bring – before shooting starts. Write down your shooting schedule. It sounds like homework, but that's only because it *is* homework.

The Technology 22

Want to know what it takes to get rolling right away? Having a camera's a good start. Buy, beg, or borrow, but don't steal one. You won't need the latest and greatest. A 20-year-old camera can do the job nicely. A videotape is also useful, and so are a few other essentials to get before you get started.

The Technique 24

Do yourself a favor. Do your audience a favor. Learn the basics of holding a camera, moving a camera, zooming the lens, controlling the sound, controlling the light, and controlling your stomach when it starts grumbling. You won't believe the difference a little learning will make.

The Special Effects 40

You may not have the *Star Wars* budget of George Lucas, but you can have his imagination. With real-time visual effects, sound effects, and camera tricks, you'll shock and amaze everyone. Especially yourself.

The Burden of Leadership

44

Remember the days when directors screamed through megaphones and carried little whips? Neither do we. Camera skills and writing skills are important, but directing is also about people skills. Use them (the skills) or lose them (the people).

The Final Touches

46

Once you've got everything you need on tape, you're mostly done. Now comes the polishing part. Final editing helps the pieces come together. Adding music, titles, and other effects will help make your mild-mannered movie a marvelous masterpiece.

The Big Show

54

Premiere means "first," so be sure your first show is first class. Make invitations. Make posters. Make popcorn. Make them be quiet. You've put a lot of time into your video. Keep them in their seats without using glue.

> YOUR OSCAR-NIGHT SPEECH
> Run up to the stage. Cry a lot. Say something political with your fist in the air. Remember to thank "the little people" who made your success possible. Then run like the wind as you're chased down the street by little people.

COOL!

Thinking in Video

Let's get a couple of things straight. First of all, this book is going to use the words *video* and *movie* to mean the same thing. Even if your video isn't a movie, it's boring to read the word *video*, *video*, *video* over and over and over. So, whatever you make will be a video *and* a movie.

Next thing to know is that a video is really a lot of still pictures (*frames*) seen in a fast sequence. How fast? Try 30 frames per second, 1,800 frames per minute, 108,000 frames per hour. When you're done watching a three-hour movie about can openers, you've seen 324,000 single images. That's a lot of can openers. No wonder you're hungry.

Video camera or still camera

Dare we compare? Lighting and composition (setting up your shot) are similar. But still cameras get blurry when you move too quickly ... and video cameras make the viewer feel blurry when you move too quickly.

Since a video is lots of still images, can you get action from still pictures? You bet – in fact, that's how it all started. The earliest motion pictures were flip books, a stack of drawings or photos with each image just a little different from the one before it. Riff the stack with your thumb and *presto*! Action without lights or camera. The Animatic and Storyboard sections will tell you more.

But it's easier to use a video camera: your talent won't have to play "freeze tag" with your still camera, and you won't have to draw lots of little running stick figures for your flip book.

You are always telling a story

Here's another word you'll see a lot here: *story*. Remember that you are always, always telling a story with your video camera. Every second of your video has to help tell that story, or else it doesn't belong. Your audience will be (a) bored or (b) confused or (c) both. Keep your story in mind every moment you shoot. It's the second-oldest rule in movies (after "use a camera").

What's that? You think you don't know how to tell stories with video? Sure you do. You've probably seen so many movies, TV shows, music videos, and commercials that you know the basic rules of visual storytelling without even realizing it. (See "What You See is What They Get" on page 28 for more clues.)

Some basic rules of visual storytelling

▪ **What is happening?** What do you want your viewer to do? Laugh? Cry? Scream? Be impressed with you? Always think about what your audience is thinking.

▪ Everything you shoot is a choice. Are you making choices that make sense for your particular video? Do they match the feeling you're trying to get?

▪ *Are you telling the story?* Are the characters, words, actions, settings, props, and effects helping tell the story, in big or little ways?

▪ Pay attention to the *frame* (the borders of the rectangle that will be the edges of your TV screen). Everything should enter, exit, or stay in the frame for a reason.

▪ Whatever you're shooting is your *subject*. It can be a person or a tree. The viewer should always know who or what the subject of your video is.

▪ Movies are about something *happening*. And something has to move – your subject or your camera. Storytelling is action.

▪ Move the camera sloooowly when you move it. (Lots more on that later.)

That's just the beginning, but it's a good start. Now that you know a few rules, it's time to start thinking about the video YOU want to shoot.

What's the Big Idea?

If someone asks what your video's about, your answer is called the *concept*. If you can describe it in one sentence, that's the concept. *The Terminator meets Godzilla* is a concept. So is *Batman's mom cleans the Bat Cave and throws out his comic books*. And so is *Two girl detectives discover their friend is a spy*. What more can we say? Write your movie's concept before going to the next step.

Concept-O-Matic™
It's easy to do! You can, too!
"My video is about what happens when …"

Start with a story:
Owen is cut from the team.

Add a prop: Owen breaks his leg.

Add characters:
Owen sits out football practice.

Add setting:
Owen sits out the big game.

Choices, choices

What you shoot depends a lot on what you have available. Are you interested in exploring the real world or in making up worlds of your own? Think about the story you want to tell and a feeling you want to share. Or do you just like acting silly in front of the camera?

Fake Out

Fictional Video Ideas

SHORT STORIES
Plan ahead. Shoot with a script. Keep it short.

IMPROVISED
No script. Stories and comedy made up on the fly.

TV SHOWS
Talk shows, game shows, or imitate your favorite show.

MUSIC VIDEOS
Sing a song or sing along.

FAKE COMMERCIALS
Make fun of TV ads. If it smells, it sells.

EXPERIMENTAL FILMS
Usually more fun to make than to watch.

Get Real

Real-Life Video Ideas

A SIMPLE PROCESS
A great place to get started. (see pages 14–15)

BIOGRAPHY
Interview someone you know, or someone you don't.

NEWS
If it happened, what's the story?

SCHOOL
Sports, clubs, events, a year-end video yearbook.

EVENTS
Parties, parades, plays, practical jokes, etc.

REALITY
The actual adventures of you and your friends.

NATURE
The amazing tricks your pet can do. Or watch cheese get moldy.

VIDEO DIARY
You, your life, even your summer vacation.

FULL TEAM AHEAD

So you're the director. In Hollywood, directors make the decisions because they're the experts. At your house, you're the director because you've got the camera. But that's no reason to hog all the fun. If you don't let the other kids share the pleasure, you'll end up videotaping the flowers out back. All alone.

Like most of us, you probably have one or three friends to shoot with. That means people will be doing double duty behind the camera (*crew*) and in front of the camera (*talent*). Since everyone can't hold the camera, you'd better know what other jobs to offer instead.

One Live Crew

Here's a list of essential roles for making a video. Sometimes just a few people do everything. And if you're going to do everything, you might as well find out what you're called.

WRITER – in charge of the story

DIRECTOR – the visionary who controls and manages the movie's creation

CAMERA OPERATOR – sets up, operates, and deals with the camera

SOUND PERSON – deals with all aspects of microphones and capturing sound

GAFFER – in charge of the lighting and related visual solutions

GRIP – in charge of sets, main props; sometimes helps the camera operator

STYLIST – in charge of costumes, makeup, actors' props

TALENT – those who work in front of the camera

EFFECTS – creates and executes the special effects

EDITOR – puts all the pieces together at the end

PRODUCER – supervisor, also known as "a responsible adult"

CATERER – see Producer

TRANSPORTATION – see Producer

EXECUTIVE PRODUCER – a producer who provides funds or very good food

STUDIO CHIEF – the owner of the camcorder

TIP

Everyone in your movie should know they're in your movie. No hidden cameras! Get people's permission before you videotape them.

GOING SOLO

What's that? Your crew is home doing homework? Relax, Hitchcock ... solo projects don't have to make you psycho:

Keep it simple. Don't bite off more than you can shoot.

Plan ahead. Plan ahead. Plan ahead. Plan ahead.

Travel light. All you really need is a camera, a blank videotape, charged batteries, a charger (just in case), a camera bag to keep things safe, and a shot list in case you want to know what you're doing.

Non-fiction videos especially lend themselves to solo shooting: interviews, events, and nature videos.

If you've got fiction on your mind, puppets, dolls, and hands make surprisingly well-behaved actors. You'll have to do the talking, though. Or, set up the camera somewhere stable and strut your stuff onscreen.

The Talent

Who's the biggest ham on camera? The actors are called talent, but that's no guarantee of actual talent.

Casting means choosing the right actor for each part. If there are only two of you, it also helps to be a master of disguise. If your video has a script, encourage your actors to memorize their lines before the shoot. It's all right if they change their lines if the changes make sense for the movie.

Enough Reading! Let's Make a Video!

Ready? Get set ... grab your camera! Get a videotape that fits in the slot. Find the red REC button. Aim the camera at something. Sooner or later hit the REC button again to stop taping. Rewind. Match the colors on your audio/video cord plugs with the colors of the jacks on your TV or VCR. Figure out how to get video to play on the TV. Sit and watch. Cool, huh?

Go ahead and satisfy that itchy recording finger. Let practice make perfect, then come back to the book for your next steps up the video ladder.

GET ROLLING!

Becoming a powerful director requires exercise. Here's an exercise. It may not be *Planet of the Grapes*, but it's a start.

Videotape a *simple process*. A what? Here are some examples:

■ making a sandwich
■ mowing the lawn
■ washing the dog
■ giving a wet dog a sandwich on the lawn

As the director/cameraperson, pretend you are invisible. Just let the action happen on its own, so it seems as natural as possible. You can let the camera stay in one place or try close-ups, wide shots, and different angles to help tell your story.

The simpler and shorter the process, the better. Here's what you can accidentally learn by making

First Steps in Planning

Have a brainstorming party: Get your people together to share ideas.

Agree on what's possible: Don't try to do what you can't do. Without a parachute, you can't get that aerial zoom shot you want. If you don't own the camera, forget the scuba-diving movie. But if you're not trying to damage the equipment or yourself, a lot of choices await you.

Add up equipment and resources:

- What brains and muscle are available?
- What gear can you get?
- Are extra lights necessary?
- Do you have enough gaffer's tape? (Duct tape.)
- What can you build?
- What can you borrow?
- What do you need to buy?
- What can replace the thing you don't have, so you can still tell your story?

TIP

Everybody has an idea. You should listen to them all, no matter how stupid they seem at first. (Or, if you're going solo, don't argue with yourself.)

simple process videos:

- how to show the individual steps of doing something
- how to capture a series of nice-looking shots
- how to match one shot to the next so it all fits together and looks right in the end
- how to work with talent (even hungry, wet dogs)

When you are done, you will have told a short story on video. It will probably be only a minute or two long. Later on, we'll get into the details of storytelling. For now, just get the feeling. Then plug it in, watch the results, and decide what you'll do differently, or the same, next time.

Ready for more? Then power down the camera and read up.

From Brainstorm to Story

Writing for video is not so scary when you go step by step. One writing tool you might not have thought about is … the video camera. Turn it on and point it at people. Use it as a rehearsal monitor. Work out your story ideas. Work out the main parts of the movie: plot, settings, characters. Try out some dialog – if it works, keep it. And using the tape, you can create your storyboard or script. Go back later and write down what you like. First stop: the plot.

The plot

In the beginning, there was the one-sentence concept. The plot is the next step – a little longer, but equally important. It's the description of what's happening, and what's at stake for the characters. A plot may take a full minute to describe while a concept takes five seconds. Write out your plot as a short story of a few paragraphs, until it's a story you can get excited about.

The setting

The setting is where the video takes place. It could be a bedroom or a planet, depending on your story. (Or both.) It could be in the year 1863 or 94965. Your imagination is the only limitation. A short movie might have only one setting, but longer movies almost always have more. If the setting is at night, try to make sure the sun doesn't peek through a window. See "Location, Location, Location" on page 20 for a little more encouragement here.

The characters

Your characters are the people in your story. Maybe they're real, maybe they're *a little like* people you know, maybe they're fungus monsters from the earth's core. That's up to you. In every story, we want to know what happens to the characters. Every character's story should have a beginning (they rise out of the ocean), a middle (they tear apart your bedroom. "Honest, Mom, it wasn't me!"), and an end (your mother tells you to put down that camera and do your homework).

Even if their stories are not the most important, make sure they do something memorable. Your video will be as interesting as its characters. Think about how many movies have left you thinking, "Who cares about those people?" That is, if you care to think about them at all.

In a documentary, the talent are real people with real stories. But what happens to them will be just as interesting if you let their stories come out naturally. Don't push … coax! If you let your real-life characters be natural, they may not look like they're selling cola on TV, but they'll be much more interesting.

The dialog

"Hey, you!" "Me?" "Yeah, you!" "What do you want?" "What do I want??" "Yeah." "Um, I don't remember. Forget it." "I already did."

Welcome to the world of dialog. Dialog is the conversation between characters in your story. It's the place where they tell you things about themselves, and the audience learns what's going on in the story. Think about your characters and what makes them tick. Get inside their heads. What would they say in the imaginary situations you put them in?

The script

If you're comfortable with the idea of writing a script for your story, it doesn't have to be hard. Most scripts have all the things you just read about – setting, characters, dialog – plus details like sound effects and camera angles. But mainly it will have the dialog. There's an example on page 57.

If you're not ready to sit and write it all down, maybe you'd be happier making a storyboard. Yeah, a storyboard. Hey, what's a storyboard?

The Storyboard
What's a storyboard?

Glad you asked. The storyboard is a tool the movie director and crew use to imagine how the movie will look *before* it is made.

A storyboard looks a lot like a comic book. Each square is a drawing that shows you what the camera will see, from the moment the director yells "Action!" until the director yells "Cut!" In the next square, which would normally be a new camera set-up, you visualize the change of camera angle and position, and the action continues. Sometimes in one minute there will be several shots (and therefore several drawings). Other times the camera might not move for a minute or more, so you'd only need one drawing to represent it.

Next to each drawing you place the matching dialog words, as well as camera set-up and production notes to help you and your crew visualize what the camera will do, what will happen onscreen, and what you will hear on the soundtrack.

"Hey, you!"
"Me?"
"Yeah, you!"
"What do you want?"
"What do I want?"
"Forget it."
"I already did."

TIP

The less talking you have, the better your actors will look! Actions speak louder than words anyway. Definitely don't use the actors to explain the plot: "Mom, remember when I had a secret map and I buried it under the garage so the zombie dude next door wouldn't find the family treasure that Grandpa hid after he invented the giant robot? Well, I lost it." You might as well have your actor sing a lullaby; your audience is fast asleep.

Why you need to make a storyboard

- lets you see the film better in your mind, so you can fix problems before shooting starts

- helps you figure out the best camera angles

- helps you be prepared before and during the shooting

- helps you get away without writing a script

- helps you show off your best stick figures

How to make a storyboard

Let's say you're filming a movie called *The Incredible Killer Sweater from Outer Space*. Here are the steps to making your own storyboard:

Draw a page with four boxes on it.

Label the boxes *Shot 1, Shot 2, Shot 3,* and *Shot 4*.

The first box is your first shot of the movie, **Shot 1**. It is a medium shot (see page 29 for shot types) of a sweater flying through the air and landing on a chair. You can't see who threw it. Write next to the box, *Add ominous swooshing sound effect as sweater flies through air.*

In the box for **Shot 2** you draw a person walking into the room from a wide angle. Next to the box write, *Footsteps can be heard as Bernie enters the room from left side of screen.*

In **Shot 3** you draw the person finding the sweater from a medium shot. Next to the box write, *Bernie wonders out loud, "Now how did this sweater get over here?"*

In **Shot 4** you draw the person putting on the sweater using a close-up on their head and shoulders. Next to the box write, *Add scary music in the soundtrack.*

Of course, on the next page you'll have four more boxes. That's where Bernie struggles with the alien sweater monster. Then you show him crushed by the sweater and lying dead on the floor. Dead Bernie is next to the sweater. Then the sweater (tied to invisible fishing line) is pulled across the floor off camera.

You see? Making a killer storyboard is no sweat.

WHAT? I CAN MAKE A MOVIE WITHOUT A CAMCORDER?

If you can't get a video camera but you have a computer set-up, some technical knowledge, and maybe a still camera, you can make movies.

Plan: Come up with a simple concept. Make a storyboard. Number each shot. Write a short script if there's any talking.

Collect: Open a folder in your computer to collect the images you need for your story. Where are the images coming from?

SAY CHEESE: Take a series of still photos of your actors doing each action that helps tell the story. If you used a digital camera, then load the images to your hard drive. If you used film, get it processed at a place that provides digital images on a CD (or online). Or, scan your prints to create digital files of the shots you want.

NO CAMERA? Use existing photos, magazine pages, drawings, or anything else, and scan them into your computer.

NO SCANNER? Use a simple drawing or painting program to whip up the images you want for your story. Now they're ready to go.

Speak: Hook a microphone to the computer. You (and any actors) can record the script. Save these lines of dialog onto your hard drive as a series of audio files.

Organize: As you create and file the image and audio files, use the same numbers to match your storyboard frames. This keeps your files in order when editing. For example, 01audio (which starts with "Once upon a time …") will end up next to 01image (a picture of a castle) in your folder. And so on. A very tidy way to go. Start at 01, 02, 03 instead of 1, 2, 3 … or the 11th file will end up next to the first. Trust us.

Cleanup: Select the dialog files you want to keep. Edit your photos or storyboard images. You can crop, change the colors, or add cool special effects.

Hey! We recommend you get help from an adult for the next steps.

Install: Go find a computer with video editing software. If that's not available, ask the computer's owner to download and install some demo or free-ware video editing software onto your computer. (Go to a search engine like Google.com and type in *video editing free-ware.*) **GET PERMISSION TO DOWNLOAD TO SOMEONE'S COMPUTER.**

Import: Import the edited dialog and images into the video editing software. You can also add music along with the dialog.

Edit: Sound goes first. With the editing software, arrange all the sound elements (dialog, narration, and music) in a *timeline* (in order) until you're happy. Then arrange the visual images in your editing timeline to match up with the sound-track. View and listen, tweak and twack, until you have a movie you are proud of.

Output: When you are done editing, output your master-piece to a digital video file. You can post it on your website or, with the right equipment, burn a DVD or make a videotape. All with no video camera!

Professional moviemakers use this technique to explore a movie idea before they shoot it. It's called an *animatic*, which is basically a storyboard on video with a soundtrack. All big-budget special effects features start out as animatics.

PLANNING

BE SMART, NOT UNSMART

Avoid shooting where there are hazards, like traffic or ladders or deer hunters. (Especially if you are starring in the new *Bambi*.)
If you ask an adult or two to help supervise your shoot, they can make sure everyone is safe while you focus on the shooting.

HMMM... HOW ABOUT A PIRATE ADVENTURE SET ON AUNT BETTY'S SAILBOAT?

They Call It Pre-production

Pre-production is the official name. Planning's the game. Once you've figured out your story, you'll save a lot of time with a little planning. And believe us, moviemaking takes plenty of time. (You think this is all going to happen one day after school? Two words: For Getit.) Doing it right means taking your time (maybe days, maybe a week or more) and respecting your team's time. Planning makes it all go more smoothly.

The more you plan, the happier your team will be at the end of the shoot, and the better your movie will turn out. It's been proven about 40,000 times.

Or ignore this advice and grab the camera and go wild. Your choice.

Location, Location, Location

Which came first – the ghost story about the floating head or the spooky house to shoot it in? That house is the location of your video. If you live in a house that inspires floating-head stories, that's your problem. If you don't, your problem is called location scouting. You have to find the creepy house, find the (possibly) creepy owners, and, creepiest of all … gasp! … get permission.

Make your life easy: shoot in locations where you can easily get permission. Choose your locations based on your story, but also base your story around the locations that are easy to work in. It's better to change a few ideas than to send the entire crew to Mount Everest to bring your vision to life.

Props and Costumes

The story calls for a mean sheriff, a brave cowgirl, and the three-legged dog who saves her. Where are you going to get them?

OK, your Aunt Greta has the western hats and the boots. Actors' clothes are called *costumes*.

Your cousin Vidalia has the rope and the toy gun. *Props* are all the things you see on camera that actors use or need. A phone, a coffee cup, a laser-guided missile launcher – these are all props.

But forget turning the neighborhood dog into "Hopalong."

HOW TO MAKE HERE LOOK LIKE THERE

Some suggestions to jump-start your imagination (and annoy the principal). Creative camera angles can really fool the eye.

School cafeteria = prison cafeteria
Furnace room = 1950s space station
Sandy beach = the vast Sahara
Nurse's office = hospital room
Principal's office = torture chamber
Garage or basement = mad scientist's lair
Old buildings = the past
New buildings = the future
Tree house = secret fortress
Lawn (super close up) = the jungle
Toilet (super super close up) = the ocean

Prop up your budget

You can avoid buying props and costumes by (1) asking people to donate them and (2) making a movie that only uses things people already own. Why bother shopping? Make a list of all the things people promised to bring. Remind them the day before. This way, they might actually bring what you need to the shoot.

Be creative and improvise with what you find at home. Look in your attic or closets for old family clothes from a bygone era of 10 or 100 years ago. If you can't find or borrow everything you need, try tag sales/garage sales and thrift stores. Stay away from expensive items and Dumpsters.

Working backwards

Finding old clothes and props could inspire your whole movie. Thin ties? Jackets without collars? Whoa – the 1980s! Can you believe what they wore in the days before DVDs? You've got a time-machine story there. Get writing!

GULP!

Camera!!!

And now, believe it or not, we're actually going to pick up the camera.

Don't be intimidated by your camcorder. Manufacturers put tons of features into camcorders to make you feel like you're getting a lot for your money. And they change those features every year so you'll buy a new one. But the most important features are the same on every camera, and those features are the ones to really know and use.

If you ever get lost navigating your way around all the buttons and knobs, remember *RTM – Read The Manual*. Your camera manual is filled with great technical secrets, and some not-so-secret things. It can help you figure out most of your questions without having to run to some adult who didn't read the manual either.

Camera Don'ts and Don'ts

Don't forget to get permission to use it.

Don't drop it.

Don't get it wet.

Don't pick it up by the tripod or use it to open walnuts.

Don't touch it with dirty, greasy, foody hands.

Don't swing it around in a china shop.

Don't leave it unattended near crooks and bad guys.

Don't do anything else dumb.

Don't.

Everything You Need to Know About Using the Camera

Shooting video is not too difficult – IF you don't push any buttons that you're not sure of. RTM if you get stuck. Here are the key concepts:

Feel the power

Make sure the batteries are full of juice, including your spare. Now turn on the camcorder.

Get set

Most camcorders let you choose between record mode and playback mode. Depending on your model, *record* may also be

HAS ANYONE SEEN THE BATTERY CHARGER?

BATTERIES

called *REC*, *camera*, or *movie* mode. *Playback* is sometimes called *play* or *VCR* mode. When the switch is set to *record*, you'll be recording as soon as you press the red REC button, which should be under your thumb.

Tape it

Without getting too technical, if you don't put a tape in your camcorder, the cam won't cord. There are a number of competing tape formats out there. Each one claims it's the best. We can tell you the truth: the best tape format is the one that fits your camcorder.

It's always better to use a new tape and have a spare on hand in case you run out. But if you must recycle, make sure you aren't recording over Aunt Eileen's kidney surgery video (unless that's what you want). Use playback mode to view your recorded tape. Fast-forward or rewind to the next place you want to start recording on the tape. Then switch back to record mode when you are ready to start taping.

Insta-Light

If your camera comes with a built-in light, the good news is that you won't always need extra lighting. The bad news: it will drink your battery dry. Bring a spare, and use the light wisely. More about lighting later (see page 33).

Sound thinking

Your camera's built-in microphone isn't meant for long distances, loud places, or windy days. (It's also not meant for spreading peanut butter on rye bread.) If you're doing a simple shoot with nearby talent in a somewhat quiet place, your camera's mic will do the job. Otherwise you might want to think about an extension mic. We'll explain that later too (see page 38).

Take aim

Point the camera at your victim. Most video cameras have automatic focus (keeping the blur away) and automatic exposure (deciding how much light you need), so you don't have to worry about setting them yourself. (Except for special situations that this book will never discuss. RTM for more details.)

Shoot

Press the record button to start recording. Press it again to stop recording. You captured your shot.

OK. Those are the basic basics. Now what?

CURRENT TAPE FORMATS

No fooling, here are the consumer video options in 2004:

8mm
Hi-8
Digital8
VHS
VHS-C
S-VHS
DV (Digital Video)
Mini DV (smaller DV)
Micro MV (Mini Video)
MiniDisc
DVD-RAM
Betamax ...
and probably 40 other letter/number combinations. One thing's for sure: by the time you read this, three formats will be off the list and five more will be on it. Don't fret that you lack the latest and greatest. The difference isn't that important.

THE TECHNIQUE

Great Idea

Practice makes perfect

Record some practice shots with your camcorder and play them back on TV. Then turn on your favorite movie and watch for tilting, panning, and other motion shots to see how your camerawork compares.

Great Idea

Use a dolly for tracking shots

When you want the camera to move a distance (say, while people walk and talk), you need a dolly. A baby's dolly gets pushed in a carriage. A professional dolly is like a railroad track. You push the camera along the rails on a cart. Instead of building a railroad, here's something just as good for rolling that camera along.

Dolly 1 Borrow a wheelchair or a chair on wheels (with permission, of course). Sit with the camera while your teammate pulls or pushes the chair. Hallways are very flat, perfect for smooth dolly shots. Watch those stairs!

Dolly 2 Dust off your little red wagon. Sit inside and hold the camera while someone *slowly* pulls the wagon. Use the flattest possible surface, like a paved driveway. For smoother shots, keep your elbows up: your arms will absorb some bumps. Make sure you don't fall off the wagon.

How to Hold Your Camera

If your camera has an image stabilization feature, turn it on, unless you are shooting an earthquake on a budget. As the name implies, this magic feature helps keep things steady even if you have hiccups. Use it.

Slow, smooth motions

Yo! This part is important. Don't make your audience seasick. You need to practice your camera moves until they are very smooth. Be sure the camera is steady and recording for at least two seconds before you move it in any direction.

After tape is rolling, start moving the camera in a single smooth motion. Keep a constant slow speed as you *tilt* (camera up and down) or *pan* (camera side to side). Then come to a smooth, slow stop before ending the shot. Always pause for two seconds before pressing the button (you will need that tape later for editing or for setting up the next shot).

It's wise to use a tripod (or one of the other "pods" described on pages 25–27). That's the easiest way to get pro-looking camera moves without the shakes. Pod that camera!

BE A POD PERSON

In case you haven't heard, keep that camera steady until you want it to move. Here are ways of not moving. Pick a position that's comfortable.

Tripod

Three legs is the steadiest way to shoot. Most tripods have a handle to let you tilt and pan the camera once it's attached. Loosen the knobs before moving the camera, and tighten the knobs to lock the camera in place for a still shot. Whenever you move the tripod to a new set-up, remove the camera first and move it separately. The little screw isn't that dependable, so don't bet your camera on it. When you set up, make sure all three legs are locked before re-attaching your camera; otherwise *Boom! Crash!* Hey! it's time to buy a new camera.

Monopod

A monopod's like a walking stick that attaches to the camera. It keeps the camera from moving up and down but not side to side. Adjust to height, lock the pod, spread your feet or kneel, and hold it steady.

Minipod

These tiny tripods can fit in your pocket. They don't cost a lot. Attach the camera and set it on a flat surface like a table. Or fold the legs together and use it as a handle.

Kneepod

We propose you get down on one knee for a steady shot. Put the camera or your elbow on your knee. Don't sneeze.

Wallpod

Lots of professionals go steady against walls and doorways. It keeps them stable.

Chairpod
Sit the wrong way and take aim. Drives teachers crazy and makes the shot steadier, too.

Floorpod
Get on the ground and lie still. If you don't fall asleep, the camera won't shake.

Friendpod
Some friends bend over backwards for you. Others will bend forwards. Lean on one for a semi-steady shot.

TIP

Don't ignore proven ideas.

Master the rules before you try to break them.

GOOD

HORIZON DOWN LOW

PERSON ON RIGHT

GOOD

HORIZON UP HIGH

PERSON ON LEFT

BAD

EVERYTHING IN THE CENTER

What You See is What They Get

Get framed

When you look through the viewfinder, you frame your shot before you start to shoot.

You don't always have to move the camera to get your frame right. Use your zoom to set up your shot. The W is *wide angle*, far back, and T is *telephoto*, zoomed up close. For best results, keep in the middle of this range, maybe a bit closer to wide angle. If you zoom too far, note that less light can get into the camera.

You're a composer

Like a painter, anything you put in the frame has an effect on your viewer. How you *compose* or arrange your frame will help tell your story. People up close look intense. People far away look lonely. Someone who enters from off-camera can add surprise. (So can a flying pie.) Experiment with these visual tools. Every time you watch a movie or TV, see how they do it. You can even call it homework.

Tic-tac-toe

There's a simple rule for composing called The Rule of Thirds. Imagine a tic-tac-toe board on your frame.

▪ People's eyes should be about level with the top line across.

▪ The horizon or landscape line should be along either the top or bottom line.

▪ Put actors and key props or buildings along either of the two vertical lines.

▪ The Dead Zone is not just a Stephen King story; it's also the middle box on your grid. It's called that because it's a boring place. Nobody, and nothing important, should stay there for long. Keep your movie edgy. Keep things along the edges.

28   *The Technique*

The Camera Shot List

To the right is a camera *shot list*. It's a list of all the camera shots in the future hit movie *Night of the Nurse*. If you make a shot list like this, your shoot will go much easier because your crew will know what to expect. All the initials will be explained after.

This shot list features most of the basic camera moves you can make. Look closely. No shot is random. Each camera angle works to help tell its part of the story. And since the shots are helping tell the story, there's no need for much dialog.

Calling the shots

Use these initials on your own shot list. You'll learn them quickly. It'll take more time to learn how each of these shots can help make your story more powerful for your viewers. But it's really worth the time.

NIGHT OF THE NURSE

(ES) A building at night. The lights are on in the building.

(LS) The front door opens – our hero, a nurse, walks out and turns. She suddenly stops.

(MS) A sound! She reaches into her purse for something.

(CU) Her face shows fear as she looks around. We hear footsteps come closer.

(LS) Cut to the street-light shadow of a person walking slowly.

(P) The camera pans to the right, following the shadow until we reach its source: the legs and waist of a police officer.

(CU) A sigh of relief comes over our hero. She smiles.

(T) Tilt up from the legs to the officer's face. It's not the police. It's a uniformed werewolf!

(CA) Our hero's hands pulling a dog whistle from her purse.

(CU) She puts the whistle to her mouth.

(MS) Officer Werewolf covers his ears in pain.

(LS) The werewolf falls to the ground under the street light.

(CU) We see our hero's face as she screams, "No! No!"

(ZO) Zoom back from her face to see she's kneeling by the body – the dead werewolf is now a human policeman on the ground. She obviously loved him.

(TS) A different angle of our hero kneeling over the body. Hold a moment, then the camera tracks further and further back, and they get smaller and smaller.

(FO) Fade to black.

(ES) Establishing shot

Also called a *wide shot*, it's used to start a new scene. It "establishes" where the action is taking place (a city, a lake, a building, a field). Think of all the movies that begin with a city skyline or a faraway shot of the school where the action will take place.

Establishing shot

Long shot

Medium shot

Close-up

(LS) Long shot

Show your talent from head to toe. Give us a look at the subjects from a slight distance without feeling too close to them. Good for introductions to characters and how they act in their world.

(MS) Medium shot

This is one of the most common shots, showing your talent from head to waist, like on a talk show. You can show one or two actors, or do an over-the-shoulder shot showing one side of a conversation.

(CU) Close-up

Head and shoulders, or even closer. This helps viewers really connect with the character, feeling his emotions. A lot of dialog is shot with "in your face" close-ups. Try an extreme close-up (ECU) showing just the eyes, which adds tension.

(P) Pan

When you pan, the camera pivots horizontally on the tripod, to the left or right. This gives viewers the feeling of looking for something and then finding it. Keep the camera motion slooooow and smooth.

The Technique

(T) Tilt

To tilt, the camera pivots vertically on the tripod, up or down, head to toe or toe to head. Again, move as smoothly as possible.

(CA) Cutaway

Cutaway shots cut from the action to a detail and back, to reveal information to your viewers. They tell the story by hiding information and then revealing it in little bits. Say you see a sleeping dog. Cut away to a torn-up, empty box of dog biscuits on a table. Cut back to the sleeping dog and you get the big picture.

(TS) Tracking shot

In the tracking shot, you and the camera are traveling together. Walking's OK, but a dolly (wheels) will be smoother. See page 24 for how to do it.

(FO) Fade-out

A fade-in (FI) occurs when the image slowly goes from black to light at the beginning of a scene, and a fade-out goes from light to black at the end. Newer cameras have all kinds of interesting fading gimmicks, usually on a button. They're fun, but they almost never help tell the story. Use sparingly.

Tilt

Zoom Out

(W) Wipe

We don't use a wipe in *Night of the Nurse* (see page 29), but you've seen them often. That's when the next scene pops out of the last scene in a burst of technology. Maybe the new scene drops in from the top like an elevator coming down. Or a spiral twists, changing the old scene to the new one. Or the old image splits and opens like an elevator door, and inside the elevator is the new scene. There are lots of wipe effects in cameras, at the push of a button or two. They're fun to try, but if you go crazy with them, so will your audience.

(ZO) Zoom Out

Or (ZI) Zoom In. This is probably the most abused trick among new video directors. Use it wisely. Use your zoom mainly for setting up your shot before you shoot, not while recording.

As an effect, directors use snap zooming mainly for shock. *Zoop!* A snake in the cereal bowl! Sometimes, slow zooming can tell the story: Start close on your subject (a girl reading a comic book) and then slowly zoom wide to let us see what's really happening in the big picture (she's playing outfield in a softball game and the ball is landing behind her). It's strange to watch a zoom because our eyes don't move like that naturally. Don't zoom too much or viewers will zoom away.

The Technique

Let There Be Lighting

For video, there's nothing more important than light. Without light, you might as well play a music tape. Today's camcorders do a great job in low light or bright light. A few new ones even shoot at night. By learning a little how light works with video, you'll not only avoid mistakes, you'll shine!

Don't mix and match light

Different kinds of light glow in different colors (see "Baby, Fire My Light" on page 37). Your camera can adjust to the color of the light because it has an automatic white balance feature. That means it works to make white things look white, even if there's yellowy light on them. Then all the other colors shift, too.

The main rule here is: Don't mix different kinds of light in your scene. You'll drive your camera insane (a little), and it will be very obvious to your viewers that the colors, light, and tone are changing from shot to shot. Keep it consistent.

Light sources

Built-in light

Some camcorders have a small built-in light. It's good for home movies, but for your super-professional show it's better as a *fill light* than as your main *key light*. (See "Light like a pro" on page 36.)

Indoor lights

Any of the lights in your house can help your shoot. Bare bulbs are good key lights, and lampshades fill in nicely. See "Light like a pro" (page 36) and "Baby, Fire My Light" (page 37) for more indoor light ideas.

Work lights

Clip-on work lights are great because they are easy to point at your talent. They (the lights) live in garages, basements, workrooms, or hardware stores. They don't cost a lot, and they really make a difference. Get permission to borrow or buy some.

Hot shoe light

Some camcorders have a "hot shoe" – the flat, square silver attachment on top that holds an extra light. This light should sit a few inches higher than the lens. Charge it up first.

Night vision

Some camcorders have an amazing infrared "night vision" feature that lets you shoot in near darkness. Everyone will look green, so we suggest using it in secret agent, military, or outer space scenes. Stand close to your subject for it to work well.

Daylight

The sun is great for light, but it's hard to move it where you need it. And the sun decides its own schedule. Good news: it's free and plentiful. Bad news: sunlight puts deep shadows on people's faces. Cloudy skies or shade will help to soften shadows. See the "Reflect on this" tip on page 35 to erase shadows by using reflected sunlight. The pros try to shoot the whole of each scene on the same kind of day (sunny or cloudy) so it all looks the same on tape when cut together.

The Technique

Lighting problems/Lighting solutions

Problem: The mix of fluorescent and tungsten lights (see "Baby, Fire My Light" on page 37) makes your actors look half blue, half yellow, and all sick.
Solution: Turn off one type of light. Add more of the other type of light. The camera will be able to white-balance much better, bringing the actors back to health.

Problem: Direct sunlight is creating hard shadows on faces.
Solution: Have someone hold a reflector (see "Reflect on This," opposite) to shine sunlight from an angle that will brighten up the shadows.

Problem: The scary monster does not look scary enough.
Solution: You need darkness and weird shadows. A single light enhances shadows. Put a light near the floor for creepy face shadows. Light your subject from directly behind for a mysterious silhouette effect. Make the shot look dark by using very little lighting ... maybe just a flashlight that sweeps around the shot, briefly shining on the sweaty kid in the monster mask.

Problem: It's too dark to shoot inside the room.
Solution: Change rooms. Or, borrow a clip light from the workshop, clip it to the seat of a chair, and keep it aimed where you need it. Remove the shade on a table lamp to make it a better light source. (Don't burn your fingers.) Open or shut curtains to control sunlight as needed. Try using your reflector inside, to help bounce sunlight or house lights onto your subject.

Blooper: Flare out!

If a bright light (especially the sun) shines into the camera lens, you'll get a big ugly streak in your picture called a lens flare. Keep your camera and light sources separated. If your talent stands in front of a light source, blocking it from shining into the lens (makes a cool silhouette effect), beware when she steps away – major lens flare!

Blooper: Sunstroke

Never point cameras at suns. It's bad for eyes, cameras, and viewers, in that order. Don't stare at the sun reflector either, even if you did build it.

Great Idea

Reflect on This – You can control the sun! (Sort of.) Make a homemade reflector by gluing or taping aluminum foil to one side of a big piece of cardboard. Have the dull side of the foil face out. It's actually better if the foil gets wrinkled, since you want to reflect diffused (spread-out) light rather than a direct blast of sun. Have the gaffer stand next to the camera and aim the reflector's light on an actor's face, until shadows get weaker. A silver sun shield from a car can make a good light reflector too.

Sunlight Delight – The sun can be either your back-light or key light. The reflector can provide your key light or fill light. Experiment to see what looks good in the camera. You may have to remind your gaffer to stand still during the takes so you don't end up with a disco ball. Two reflectors can be better than one in some cases. If you only have one gaffer, try leaning the other reflector against a wall or tree.

No light

Key light

Light like a pro

Your best bet is to use existing light. (Translation: Shoot your video where there is already a bunch of light.) But if you want to learn lighting, here's the Hollywood way.

It's called *three-point lighting*: three lights in three different places aimed at the middle, and *presto!* they mostly erase each other's shadows. Hard shadows are bad stuff in videos, except in monster and bad-guy stories.

The three lights of this system are:

Key light – The first and brightest light, usually pointing at the subject. A work light, or a 100-watt bulb without a shade, would make a good key light.

Fill light – The second light, half as bright, is placed opposite the key light on the other side of the camera. It softens most of the shadows cast by the key light. A basic work light with a 50-watt bulb, or a lamp with a shade, can do the trick.

Backlight – The third light is set behind the talent, to help them stand out from the background. Don't shine it directly into the camera lens. A lamp (with a shade) in the background would make a good backlight for you. You can even keep it visible in the frame.

If you can't get all three lights set up, try just a key and a fill light. No? Just a key light, then. No? Use the light on your camcorder. Or the sun. Or the refrigerator light …

Key light + fill light

Key light + fill light + backlight

The Technique

BABY, FIRE MY LIGHT

It's a little advanced, but it's good to know some basic types of light, and their effect on videotape. Try not to mix them in a shot. Here they are, starting with the good and ending with the not so good.

LIGHT: Daylight
WHAT IT IS: A brilliant golden light from our local star.
GOOD FOR: Exterior daytime shooting, day-for-night shooting (see "Nighttime in daytime" on page 42), shooting inside rooms with lots of windows.

LIGHT: Halogen
WHAT IT IS: A brilliant white light bulb found in many desk and floor lamps.
GOOD FOR: Everything … Halogen mixes pretty well with daylight, too.

LIGHT: Tungsten
WHAT IT IS: The normal everyday light bulb. These regular light bulbs have a warm, yellowish light.
GOOD FOR: Shooting indoors when that's what's available. Looks "homey."

LIGHT: Fluorescent
WHAT IT IS: A blue-white light from tube bulbs.
GOOD FOR: Shooting inside schools, stores, or bathrooms, where we expect that kind of light. Usually makes people look pale or cold. Good for sick characters.

LIGHT: Neon
WHAT IT IS: Tubes filled with gas. Can be shaped to say *Open all night* or *Drive-up Window* in cool colors.
GOOD FOR: Gritty urban drama, with wailing saxophones and tough kids wearing sunglasses all night long.

LIGHT: Night light
WHAT IT IS: Shaped like a cartoon character or the moon. Good for bedrooms, lousy for video.
GOOD FOR: Finding the bathroom at night without tripping.

Remember, consistent light is better than perfect light.

TEST 1, 2, 3...

Sound Recording

Good sound is just as important as good lighting. It's frustrating to not hear the actors, and distracting noises always distract. But if you do it right, you'll hear applause from your audience.

Sound advice

- Quiet on the set!
- No heavy breathing behind the camera. No eating, either. Stop it right now.
- Get the mic as close to your talent as possible.
- Listen on headphones while you're shooting (if the camcorder has a headphone jack).
- Was that a jet overhead? Play back your takes to make sure the sound was recorded well. The time to shoot another take is before moving on to shoot the next scene.

Built-in microphones

All camcorders have built-in microphones, on top or at the front of your camera. This type of mic will pick up every sound from every direction, so don't mutter insults at the actors. For general shooting, the built-in mic is good enough … and one less thing to worry about. Some new shooters stick their fingers on or around the mic. This will sound *awful*! Hands off.

Blooper: Call me mic

You thought it should be spelled "mike," right? Well, you're a pro now, so it's "mic." But it sounds like "mike."

External microphones

If your camcorder has a mic input jack, then think about taking your sound to the next level. An external microphone makes a big difference because it brings the voice and the mic into close range. It can be a hand-held mic for interviews, or a little mic that hides on someone's shirt or a nearby prop.

You can spend a week's allowance – or a year's, depending on your allowance. Even an inexpensive mic will be a sound investment. (Get one at your local electronics megabox.)

In addition to your mic, get an extension cord of at least 10 meters (30 feet). Then you can set up your shot and have enough cord to snake back to the camera. If you don't want your mic and all that cord to be seen by the camera, your best bet is a boom (see "Make a Sonic Boom," opposite). You might be able to borrow a wireless mic from school or the opera. There's no cord to trip over, but you'll need a lesson in using one.

Testing, 1, 2, 3

Before you begin shooting, take a test. See how your audio microphone can handle any task you've got for it. Keep everything on your audio checklist ready, so no one's kept waiting.

Audio checklist

- Headphones
- Headphone extension cord if the audio person is not also operating the camera
- External mic (and any plug adapters you need)
- External mic extension cord
- Boom pole (if you're using one; see "Make a Sonic Boom," opposite)
- Extra batteries for battery-powered mics
- Audio-To-Go wagon or travel case

Make a Sonic Boom

How to keep a good mic near the action but out of sight? Build a boom mic. Connect a good microphone to a broomstick with all that duct tape you've got. Make sure your cable's long enough. A 10 meter (30 foot) audio extension should be plenty. If you have a telescoping aluminum painting pole, that's even better than a broomstick. Have someone hold the whole thing out of view, above the talent's heads, off camera. It takes strong arms and good ears. After each take, ask how the sound sounded.

Blooper: Crash and flush

Don't walk too far when headphones or microphones are wired to the camera. *Crash!* Lots of otherwise smart people forget, and wreck their equipment. Also, if you're using a wireless mic, make sure your talent turns it off before taking a bathroom break.

THE SPECIAL EFFECTS

A stampede of 200 wild horses charging through downtown. A huge ship made from trees by beavers. An intergalactic car wash. Someday you may have the chance to direct these special effects in a movie. Until then, let's see what you can do without blowing your allowance.

Some great special effects can be created while you are shooting. No computers, no animation, and no fortune required.

Live Visual Effects

No one expects your movie to look as good as a Hollywood feature, but with a little cleverness you will keep your audience (and your team) psyched. Here are a few visual tricks that are also treats:

◼ Shoot your action in a reflective surface like a car window, a mirror, a swimming pool, or other water. Then pull back to show the "real" world and continue the action.

◼ Put your camera on its side. Then pretend the floor is a wall and the wall is a floor. Whoops, did you drop something?

◼ Pretend the camera is a person. Have your actors talk to it, looking straight into the lens. Have the camera operator (or an off-screen actor) say the "camera's" lines. Let the camera take a walk. Just keep it at eye level, and don't trip over anything.

◼ Pretend the camera is a dog and the viewer sees everything through its eyes. Get down on the ground and wander. Watch that fire hydrant!

◼ Take a flexible mirror made of aluminum foil or a sheet of reflective Mylar. Hold it at a 45° angle in front of the camera lens with your subject at a 90° angle from the camera. Zoom all the way in, so that all you can see is the reflection in the mirror. Bend the mirror to achieve wavy, distorted images while shooting. Great for segments showing your character dreaming or being crazy.

Know all the angles

These effects don't take any effort at all. And they'll give you more ways to tell your story.

- Put the camera near the ground and point up. Low angles make things look taller, and make bad guys look badder.
- Put the camera up high and point down. Make a character seem weak, small, or in danger. Make a toy building look real (depending on the toy).
- Show your characters against the sky, with no other background. They'll look like they're on a mountaintop.
- Show a character. Cut away (see the example opposite) to a beehive, or a python, or a cafeteria lady. Now cut back to the character, who looks scared, right? Your viewers add up the different pieces for extra impact. Now replace that python with a birthday cake. The footage of the actor is identical, but you'll swear the character is thinking about blowing out candles this time.

From weather to weapons

Need that perfect effect to get your story across? Here are a few favorites:

Snow job

Does your movie need a snowfall? Try instant mashed potato flakes. Frame a close-up of your hero, and have a crew member sprinkle the potato flakes just above the shot, near the lens. Is it a blizzard? An electric fan on an off-screen table makes an instant blizzard! Substitute dry leaves for the potato flakes if it's fall. Change the wind by moving your fan closer or farther away. Watch those fingers!

To show snow on the ground, don't waste all those potato flakes. Shoot winter scenes in the winter and summer scenes in the summer. *Work with what you've got* is the key to happiness and staying sane in moviemaking.

Earthquake

Put lots of things on a table. Have a few people crouch down and shake the legs while the camera operator shakes the camera *very slightly*. The actors should stumble around as if they feel the floor under them quaking. This is how they shoot the battle scenes in science fiction movies. It's low budget and it really works.

Wind, hurricane, tornado, breeze

Use a fan. Don't cut off your fingers. Period.

Rain

Aim a garden hose in front of the camera so that the camera *does not get wet*. Or hold a colander above your scene where the camera can't see it. Then pour water into the colander. The effect should look good. *Keep the camera safe and dry or you'll be wringing out your piggy bank.*

After the rain

Driveways and sidewalks look slick and dramatic when they're wet. The wet surfaces catch the light for great effect. (The lone hero always makes his final exit on a wet street.) Use a garden hose to wet the driveway or sidewalk – NOT the kitchen – and don't give control of the water to the wrong kid or you'll be hosed!

Nighttime in daytime

Need night but need to see? Use the manual exposure control to make your picture look dark. Also use the manual white balance to make the picture look blue. How? Read the manual. To make it look more convincing, shoot on a cloudy day or just after sunset to avoid hard shadows. This technique is called day-for-night shooting.

Gone and back

How do you make someone (or something) vanish? Put the camera on a tripod or completely steady surface and record your scene. At the director's hand signal (no noise, please) all action freezes and the camera operator pushes the pause button. The actor (or thing) disappears. You can also add people in the scene in the same way. This will need a little practice.

Attack props

For some reason, modern filmmakers need to make movies about characters whacking each other with solid objects. If you must go after each other with weapons, make them out of Styrofoam and color them. (When you buy a TV or computer or microwave, there's lots of good Styrofoam.) DON'T use actual hard objects, OK??

Stunts

Car chases! Kung fu moves! Jumping through a glass window! Picking up a piano and throwing it – while someone is playing it! Want to do these stunts? Here's all you have to do: drink a nice warm cup of milk, have a nap, and *dream* about them. Did you think the authors were going to tell you how to do anything even remotely like that? Stick with the Styrofoam.

The Special Effects

LAWYERS' NOTE: The authors really wanted to tell you how to do stunts. This made the lawyers laugh very hard. AUTHORS' NOTE: Camera angles, montage, and clever editing can make lame, lawyer-approved stunts look better than you'd expect. Practice, practice, practice.

Live Sound Effects

Since the glory days of radio, great live sound effects have been an art form. Make it real. Make it fun. Just don't let your sound effects drown out dialog.

Here are a few effects to experiment with:

Wind: Exhale gently through your teeth near the mic.

Explosion/Thunder: Vibrate the back of your tongue and exhale/gargle on the mic not so gently. Every kid knows how to make this noise, but it's impossible to describe.

Fire: Keep crunching and releasing a ball of plastic wrap near the mic.

Rain: Put dried beans in a tambourine drumhead and roll them slowly above the mic. First tape down the jingles so they don't jangle.

Telephone voice: Cup your hands or speak into a cup near the microphone. Let your nose vibrate as you talk. Or, put a mic against a phone and call yourself.

Background sounds: Use a portable tape recorder (like a boom box) and a mic to record the real world: nature sounds, machines, traffic, classroom sounds, lunchroom chattering, etc. Your actors could be parked in the driveway and it'll sound like they're in a car chase. Play the boom box near the camcorder while you shoot.

Pro noise: Borrow a sound effects tape or CD from your library. There are plenty to choose from, even special ones for Halloween. Or download WAV files off the Internet. From doors creaking to mice squeaking to balloons leaking, it's all waiting for you.

If you know how to edit your video after you're done shooting (see page 52), you can add the sound effects at that time, for even more options and greater sound control.

THE BURDEN OF LEADERSHIP

Direct Challenge

So you're the director. Yes, the director calls the shots. That doesn't make you the big shot, but it's big work. Treat people well or you'll be directing traffic instead. Remember, you're not an emperor – you're just the kid with the video camera. So what's in store for you?

■ Directing is a fun challenge. You get to see your ideas come to life. And you get to tell stories that are important to you.

■ It takes planning, planning, planning. Nobody wants to sit around while you make up your mind – or make up the next idea. Get it all ready before you get going.

■ Delegate. Which means, divvy up the jobs.

■ Focus, good communication, hard work – sounds like Scouting, and in a way it is. Be prepared, and be open to other people's suggestions or they won't play.

■ The director decides what stays and what goes, and should do it in a fair and smart way. Your decisions should be in the best interest of the story and of the people working with you. Not because it's your camera. Ya know?

Directing Checklist

■ Plan ahead. Write things down and make copies for your team. It *really* helps.

■ Provide clear directions to your team during the shoot.

■ Divvy up the jobs fairly and effectively.

■ Be considerate of the time and patience of your team.

■ Feed your team if it's your show. Hungry volunteers quit quickly.

■ Have backup plans if you get stuck.

■ Don't hog all the credit. It's a team effort!

Calling the Shots – The Director's Lines

Like the actors, the director has lines to say on the set. Get them right!

- **"Ready on the set"** – Let the team know you're ready to take a shot. Everyone should take their positions and be quiet and alert.
- **"Roll camera"** – Tells the camera operator (if it's not you) to start recording. She responds by saying "Rolling."
- **"Action"** – Tells the actors to start performing.
- **"Cut"** – Says the shot is over. The camera operator stops recording and everyone prepares for what's next.
- **"It's a wrap"** – Says the taping is over, or maybe that lunch is like a burrito.

Viewing the "Dailies"

Did you get what you need? If not, when else will you shoot it? During the shoot, set the camera to playback mode to rewind and see if you got the footage you want. After reviewing the shot, make sure you cue the tape to *after* the end of the last take so you don't erase that great performance. If you didn't get what you need, shoot another take. Use the headphones to be sure it sounds right.

TIP

Be smart with tape

All tapes have record tabs. They're on the long, thin end that doesn't have the spring-latch door. See it? Pop it out or slide the lock and you won't accidentally record over your work. Also, when you take a completed tape out of your camcorder, label it clearly with the date and title and important contents. That's a good time to pop the record tab, too.

SUCCESSFUL DIRECTORS MIND THEIR P's AND Q's:

Patience (it takes time)
Persistence (it takes work)
Permission (it takes the heat off)
Pleasantness (a dumb word, but we're stuck with P's here. You don't want a crew mutiny.)
Quirkiness (it takes humor to make humor)
Quality (make it a movie to be proud of)
Quickness (don't be so nuts about quality that you drive people nuts)

   Remember to keep things fun for all the people who are helping to bring your moviemaking vision to life.

IT'S PLAYBACK TIME!

THE FINAL TOUCHES

Editing Overview

The shooting's over and you're the last one standing. You've got all the footage. It's a movie now, right? Maybe, and maybe not.

Editing means selecting the best take of each shot and putting them all together (with sound, music, and any effects) to create a seamless finished show.

It may seem like putting together a puzzle the first time you edit a film. It takes experience (and equipment) to edit like the pros do. Before we get into the details of serious post-production editing, there is another, much easier and faster type of editing that you may want to try.

In-camera Editing

The in-camera editing style is the easiest and fastest way to edit. It is also the riskiest, because you could accidentally lose some work. And some hair.

For this style of production, the shooting and editing are done at the same time. Be extra careful each time you start and stop the recording during the shooting. At the end of the day you won't have a super-polished movie, but it will be finished. You get to your premiere right away! People will either say you are a genius or a slacker.

First shot (MS)

Third shot (CU)

Second shot (LS)

In-camera editing techniques

Plan your shots as much as possible in advance, using a script and/or storyboard. This means you

- Make any titles in advance on title cards. Shoot them with the camera exactly where you want them to appear in your finished movie (usually at the beginning and end).

- Rehearse each shot by going over camera moves and dialog with your team before recording a take. You'll want to use hand signals or shoulder taps with your camera operator, so you don't record your voice on the finished movie. If you're the camera operator, don't talk to yourself.

- Record long takes, and keep the camera rolling during long stretches of dialog and action. The less you start and stop the camera, the less your chances of accidentally erasing something good. Or erasing something not so good that you decided to keep anyway.

8½ steps to in-camera success

1. Shoot each shot as a single take. Include some *padding*, or extra footage, after the end of the action of the shot. You'll record over most of this padding during the next take, but it has to be there because the VCR needs a little tape every time you hit stop (like a plane needs a runway). It's tricky at first. Practice.

2. After the take, switch the camera to playback mode, rewind, and watch the previous two shots to find your new cue (start) point. If you stop too early, you'll tape over something you wanted to keep.

3. When you reach the point where you want to record the next shot, pause the tape at the end of the last shot. Go one second beyond where you want the next shot to start.

4. While still paused, switch the camera back to record mode and get ready to start the next shot in the movie. The director should call "Action" just before you press the record button so you don't record his voice on the tape.

5. If you mess up, you may have to go back and reshoot a couple of shots until you fix the mistake. Sometimes you can find a new place to end an old shot, so you can save some of it. Restart from there.

6. If you mess up enough times, your team will want to shoot you instead of the movie.

7. Repeat the steps to success until you've completed all your shots.

8. When you are done shooting, go inside and hook up your camera to a TV to give the premiere of your completed movie!

8½. Bring an autograph pen and start wearing sunglasses indoors.

TIP

If possible, use a VCR with a *flying erase head*, especially for recording, so that your edits are good and don't have a lot of "noise" (static and blurring) at the edit points. Most current camcorders and VCRs have four or more heads, including the flying erase head feature. (That's also a great name for a band.) Read the manual.

Adding polish

If you want to go back and improve your show from the start, begin with a fresh section of tape, and re-shoot all the shots as fast as possible. Practice makes perfect! It's more fun for your crew to work fast anyway, like sled dogs. Yell "Mush!" if they slow down.

Later on, if you get access to editing equipment, you can always do some post-production editing. That's where a lot of movie magic takes place.

Post-production Editing

Post-production is everything you do *after* you are done shooting. There are two editing approaches to choose from, depending on the equipment available

The Incredible Killer Sweater from Outer Space - Script - page 3

3 takes - use second (tape counter 5:33)

SHOT 08: MS
INT. KITCHEN - BERNIE'S HOUSE - SAME TIME
A sweater flies through the air and lands on a chair with an ominous WHOOSH! As it settles, we hear footsteps approaching.
SOUND EFFECTS: ominous WHOOSH, footsteps

4 takes - use last one (starts at 10:26)

SHOT 09: LS
Bernie enters the kitchen.
BERNIE: (to himself) **Now how did this sweater get over here?**
Bernie picks up the sweater and pulls it on over his head as scary music builds.
SOUND EFFECT: scary music

only one take - use it! (16:22)

SHOT 10: CU
The alien sweater monster tightens at the neck! Bernie struggles and clutches and grunts, then falls to the floor.
BERNIE: **Umph! Ugh! Argh! Oomf!**

to you. The VCR edit is doable now, while the computer edit requires so much ever-changing technology and software that we can only give you a quick overview.*

The VCR edit

This takes more patience than expertise. You need a VCR and your camera. We assume you have a VCR.

- Put the original tape with the raw footage into your camera. This will be your playback deck.
- Put a new tape in your VCR. This will be your recording deck.

Actually, we tried to get a software company to sponsor a "mention" but they wouldn't give us their money. Or their software. Or a return phone call.

- Connect them with cables. On the camcorder, connect the Audio/Video Out (A/V OUT) to the A/V IN jacks on the VCR (see diagram). They are color-coded – yellow for video, red and white for audio.
- Fast-forward or rewind on the camcorder to find each shot you want to use. Once you've found it, press play. (Start a little early for the first shot.)
- Then press record on the VCR.
- Alternate between the record and pause buttons on the VCR, because hitting stop each time is less precise.

- Repeat this until you have copied all the final shots, in the correct order, from the camcorder to the VCR.
- Now the tape in the VCR is your finished movie.

Congratulations! You have earned your own killer space sweater. Wear it carefully.

The digital video edit

The second approach is to edit digital video on a computer. There are many consumer and professional software packages for editing digital video. You'll have to research what is available and pick the best package for you. You can often get limited or trial versions free on the Internet. Get permission *before* you download anything!

The fact is, technology changes all the time. The following steps are valid today but will probably become outdated by Thursday. If any terms here seem like gibberish, sorry. There's no time to explain – it's a short book. Also, some of these terms are brand names. We aren't endorsing any specific brands, sadly.

The key items for editing digital video:

- A digital video camcorder with Firewire (IEEE 1394) digital video output.
- A powerful computer with a Firewire port.
- A special Firewire cable to connect camcorder and computer.
- Digital video editing software, such as iMovie™, Final Cut Pro™, or Premiere™. *(NOTE: It's never too late for a sponsorship, fellas.)*
- An experienced friend to help you set this up and show you the ropes of how to use the software. All video editing tools use similar concepts (which we will explain), but each also has individual ways of working that require some special training. Once again, Read the manual.
- Lots of spare time to learn and do the editing.

The fact is:

You don't need any of this stuff unless you get really serious. But if you're up for the technical challenge, and have access to the goods, read on!

EEE - EYE
EEE - EYE
OH!

Is it digital?

Unless it clearly says digital, your camcorder is analog. And that's just fine. To use digital (in-computer) editing, you only need to convert the tape. Connect your analog camcorder into a digital camcorder or VCR and record your analog tape onto digital tape. Video computer boards do something similar, but it's more complex. Read those manuals!

Firewire

Firewire is also known in the biz as iLink™ and IEEE 1394. (They say "Eye triple-E, thirteen ninety-four," but you're more likely to hum "Old MacDonald.") The widely used Firewire digital video standard was invented by Apple Computer™ to allow various camcorders and computers to easily exchange digital video. By the time you read this, this could be ancient history.

Talk to a techie

Put up some signs or ask around school to find your neighborhood video expert. Lots of kids have great editing software on their computers. One of them can take your shots and turn them into something great. Some tech types don't want to shoot video, they just like the computer biz. There's the beginning of a beautiful friendship. Pull up a chair and learn some editing basics.

Some camcorders don't use the entire audio track when they record. For instance, if yours has 16-bit audio, you can record in 12-bit mode. This leaves 4 bits (25% of the audio track) free for additional audio. Adding sound is easier that way. RTM and find out how to connect a computer or tape player to your camcorder to sweeten the sound.

Post-production: sound

You (or your friend with the audio software) can "sweeten" and mix your soundtrack. *Sweeten* means "make it sound better." Sweet.

Sound level too low or too high on your original footage? No problem. Using editing software, you can bring up the volume on the too-quiet spots and at the same time use *compression* to bring the too-loud spots down to bearable levels. You can sometimes nip this problem in the bud by using your camcorder's *limiter* or *auto-gain* features to help you keep the audio levels under control while you are shooting.

Other things you can experiment with during audio post-production:

- Add music you create or get from music libraries.
- Add sound effects you create or get from sound effects libraries.
- Record and add narration.
- Replace bad dialog mistakes.
- Remove sounds you accidentally recorded during the shoot (like that jet, or some smoker coughing off-camera).

Post-production: titles

Titles feature the name of the video and the people who made it. Titles often appear at the beginning (main titles) and end (end titles). They can be an art form in themselves, and a fun start for your video. Or you may want easy titles that just get the information across. It's your choice.

The name game

Rule #1 for short movies: Your titles should be shorter than your video. Keep your titles onscreen no longer than five seconds each, or a bit longer if there's lots written on them. Try to use as few as possible; however, a young video genius we know says, "Titles make the movie." Your call. Here are the key title cards to include:

- the movie's name (*A Bongo Family Thanksgiving*)
- the director (*Directed by Jojo Bongo*)
- the writer (*Written by Bobo Bongo*)
- the actors (*Starring Bobo, Mo, Flo & Dodo Bongo*)
- the crew's names and main job on the movie (*Camera Operator: Yoyo Bongo*)
- legal notice (*Copyright © 2009 by Jojo Bongo. All rights reserved. Any resemblance to the real Bongo family is a total freaky coincidence. No kidding.*)

HOW ABOUT... "THE AMAZING AND TRUE STORY OF LEONARD THE LABRADOR RETRIEVER WHO RESCUES A KIDNAPPED BABY FROM A RUNAWAY STROLLER"

HOW ABOUT... LEONARD THE WONDER DOG IN "STROLLER COASTER"

Don't bother listing all the jobs you did. Being credited as the director (or writer and director) says it all. Nobody cares if you were the light-bulb buyer.

Make sure one of your titles shows a legal notice to protect ownership of your work.

Fast titles

Make title cards on art board, cardboard, the pages of a pad of paper, a chalkboard, a marker board, a blank book, or use your imagination (if ink will stick to it). One friend of ours wrote titles on scraps of paper, then taped them to a window, tilting the camera down while we read.

Allow three to five seconds per title or name.

Computer-generated titles

There are lots of ways to make title cards with a computer. Make them with a word processing or illustration program and then print them out so you can shoot them with a camera. Or, you can create titles in a computer animation program and output them to digital video.

Your camcorder or video editing software may have the built-in ability to make titles. This might be your best bet if you are already doing post-production editing. Watch the spelling!

BLOOPERS TAPE

If you shot footage that has funny mistakes, edit all your goofy outtake scrap shots together to make a short bloopers tape. Or, if you have just a few funny bloopers, put them at the end, after the credits roll. Or just show the bloopers to the cast and crew. You be the judge!

*P*remiere means "first," but it comes last. It's the moment you've been waiting for. Maybe you own a long red carpet. If you do, leave it where it is.

The Premiere

■ Where to stage it? A room with a TV is a good start. If that TV is at someone else's house, your library, or your school, get permission first. Nobody likes hosting an unexpected screening.

■ Whom to invite? Your crew, your cast, your friends, your family, and anyone who helped produce the film. Ask other kids from school to come see it, plus anyone who owns a lot of unpopped popcorn.

■ How to promote it? Word of mouth. Hand out invitations to special guests. Put up posters only if the public is invited. Invite a reporter from the school newspaper (or the local paper) to the shoot and to the premiere.

■ How to make it fun? Dress up in costumes or formal wear. Serve snacks. Decorate. Put photos of the actors on a piece of cardboard; write serious or funny captions. Maybe show your bloopers tape. After your movie, tell people a couple of short, funny stories about what happened during the shoot. (And we mean *short*.) ALWAYS thank and give credit to your team. Being part of the fun is why they were there with you.

The Big Show

Hey, you made it through the book. Even the editing part. That's a good start. Did you read *every single word*? Even the copyright information? Steven Spielberg would have. Or his little people, anyway.

Actually, you don't have to be Spike Lee or Spike Jonze to have fun making a video. You just have to learn some of the basics we covered between these covers, and practice them. And keep buying videotape – don't forget that part.

Whether you want to make real documentaries or fake films, music videos or talk shows, the tools and moves are the same. Just do your best, and you'll be amazed at the results. And you'll want to keep getting better.

Keep making movies.

As we head off into the sunrise (we've been up all night writing), our publisher insists we say uplifting and supportive things to you, in order to give you self-confidence or something like that. We think you're too savvy to fall for it, but hey, they run the show.

Congratulations, you star! You're on your way! We're proud of you! It's not so hard, really. And you'll just get better each time. Once you finish a movie, start another. Try something new each time. The basics will become much easier. Learning videomaking is like learning a musical instrument. Practice! Experiment! Go for speed one time and quality the next. Learn bits about editing and you'll have a better idea what to shoot. Experiment with animation, computer graphics, and sound effects to give yourself more ways to tell your story. Always tell a story. And keep having fun.

Can you believe some people do this for a living? It's true. OK, they mainly stand on street corners with walkie-talkies, telling people they can't walk down their own street until the actors go home, but that's how you get paid in the biz while you make all your own independent movies on a shoestring budget. Are you feeling uplifted yet? See you at the movies.

– Mark and Hazlitt

(who made their first video together in 1984)

There are a bunch of different types and versions and formats of movie scripts. Since this isn't a book about scriptwriting (or baking), we won't be discussing scripts (or fluffier pancakes). We've used one of the most common formats here. We've also scribbled in our shooting notes. Your script and notes can look different, and that's OK. We're cool with diversity. Do whatever is easiest for you.

Whether or not your movie is scary, writing and shooting from a script doesn't have to be.

The Incredible Killer Sweater from Outer Space

by

Mark N. Hazlitt

TITLE CARD 01.

The Incredible Killer Sweater from Outer Space

TITLE CARD 02:

A Video by Mark N. Hazlitt

TITLE CARD 03:

Somewhere in a city like yours …

FADE TO

SHOT 01: LS & tilt

EXTERIOR. BERNIE'S HOUSE – DAY

It's a beautiful day. All we see is bright blue sky, with some white, fluffy clouds. The camera tilts slowly down, past treetops, to the roof of a house in a quiet neighborhood. A UFO zips past the tilting camera. The camera stops when it is even with the front door of the house.

SPECIAL EFFECT: Frisbee attached to white shirt box

SHOT 02: CU

The UFO settles on the lawn as threatening music sounds.

SOUND EFFECT: scary music

SHOT 03: LS & dolly We see the front of the house again. The camera dollies forward until the entire front door fills the frame. BERNIE, a skinny kid in baggy pants, opens the door and pokes his head out.

BERNIE:

SHOT 04: CU & tilt

(calling to someone in the house)
I'm sure I heard something. Maybe it was Little Jimmy teasing the cat again.

BETTY:

(off-screen)
You're hearing things. C'mon, deal the cards. You're losing.

Bernie closes the door. The camera tilts slowly from the door to a place under the bushes where the UFO is hiding. But the UFO's cargo pod is open … and empty!

INTERIOR. LIVING ROOM – BERNIE'S HOUSE – SAME TIME

SHOT 05: MS

Bernie sits down at the table where he and BETTY are playing cards. Betty has most of the poker chips. Her small glasses magnify her cranky, concentrating eyes as she expertly deals a hand. Bernie is blowing on his cards, tapping them, knocking on wood. Then he looks at them and moans.

BERNIE:

Aargh! Aargh! Oh, ick!

BETTY:

OK, I bet 50 cents.

Bernie throws down his cards. At the same moment the cards hit the table, there is a loud CRASH!

SOUND EFFECT: giant explosion

BETTY:

Don't be a sore loser, Bernie.

SHOT 06: CU Bernie's sweaty, nervous eyes widen.

BERNIE:

No, wait. That wasn't me this time. Honest.

SHOT 07: LS Bernie gets up from the table. Betty hides her cards.

BERNIE:

(muttering)
Could it be?

BETTY:

Will you get me some fish sticks while you're out there, please?

SHOT 08: MS	**INT. KITCHEN – BERNIE'S HOUSE – SAME TIME**

A sweater flies through the air and lands on a chair with an ominous WHOOSH! As it settles, we hear footsteps approaching.

SOUND EFFECTS: ominous WHOOSH footsteps

SHOT 09: LS Bernie enters the kitchen.

BERNIE:

(to himself)

Now how did this sweater get over here?

Bernie picks up the sweater and pulls it on over his head as scary music builds.

SOUND EFFECT: scary music

SHOT 10: CU The alien sweater monster tightens at the neck! Bernie struggles and clutches and grunts, then falls to the floor.

BERNIE:

Umph! Ugh! Argh! Oomf!

BETTY:

(off-screen)

Bernie! Will you stop eating all the fish sticks?

SHOT 11: CU The sweater slowly peels itself off its victim, revealing Bernie's dead face.

SPECIAL EFFECT: unseen hand pulls sweater off-screen

BETTY:

(o.s.)

And don't stick your fingers in the tartar sauce, either!

SHOT 12: LS & pan Bernie's body lies still as the sweater glides across the floor. The camera watches as the sweater creeps through the door and out of sight. We continue to watch the doorway as Betty talks from the room beyond.

SPECIAL EFFECT: unseen fishing line pulls sweater along

BETTY:

(o.s.)

**Oh, look, Bernie, the kitty is hiding in a sweater. Isn't that
cute? I guess she's hiding from Little Jimmy. Here, kitty kitty,
let me help you out of that turtleneck sweater.**

SHOT 13: LS & tilt **EXT. BERNIE'S HOUSE – SAME TIME**

The house as we first saw it, but the neighborhood is not so quiet now ...

BETTY:

(o.s.)

AAAAAAAHHHH!!!

The camera tilts up slowly back toward the sky.

FADE TO BLACK

GLOSSARY

analog video – A format that records video signals the traditional way. Any camcorder or VCR that isn't digital or DV is analog.

animatic – A series of still images with a soundtrack. Basically a storyboard on video with sound.

auto-gain – An audio feature in camcorders that sets the audio levels automatically. This can be great for having one less thing to worry about during your shooting, but pros set levels manually.

camcorder – A video camera that also holds a videotape. We frequently use the word *camera* in this book to mean a camcorder.

cast – Your group of actors. *Casting* is the action of choosing actors for your story.

compression – The practice of adjusting the sound levels on an audio track to make too-loud sounds quieter and too-quiet sounds louder.

dailies – The *raw* (not edited) footage of a day's shoot. Watching them is a filmmaking tradition. See the mistakes so you can do better next time.

delegate – To give different people different jobs to do.

digital production – Any part of the process of making a movie where the video and audio signals are stored and edited in numerical form using computers.

digital video – A new format that records video the way computers read information – as data – without loss of quality.

dolly – (1) a toy human (2) a famous sheep (3) to roll your camera toward or away from your subject on a wheeled platform. *Dolly-in* for moving closer, *dolly-out* for moving farther away.

final cut – The completed show when the director and producers agree to stop editing.

gaffer – The person in charge of rigging the lighting for the scenes and taping down cords so nobody trips.

gaffer's tape – Duct tape. Gaffers use it for everything.

grip – The person on your production team in charge of adjusting sets, lighting, and props, and who sometimes assists the camera operator.

in the can – When a film is in the can, it's 100% finished.

limiter – An audio feature in camcorders that keeps loud sounds from overloading your soundtrack during shooting.

off-camera – Outside the field of view of your camera, and not recordable.

on-camera – Within the frame of the viewfinder of your camera, and recordable.

padding – Extra footage recorded at the beginning and/or ending of a shot. Allows extra room on the tape for editing.

pod – The authors made up this term. It comes from *tripod* and *monopod* (real words), both of which stabilize your camera. We describe many other ways to pod your camera!

post – Short for *post-production*, which means everything you do after shooting ends and before the final cut. This includes editing, titles, and computer-generated effects.

premiere – The first showing of your completed masterpiece. Usually there's a party.

prop – Any visible item used by the actors is a prop.

rough cut – The first edited version of your show. Usually it is a lot longer than the final cut, since there's always more editing (cutting) to do.

RTM – Read The Manual.

script – The written document containing the dialog, details about the action, and descriptions of camera shots, camera movements, sound effects, and music.

shoot – To record on tape. Or, the action of using the camera. Or, the name of what you're all working on together.

sound effects – Imitation sounds, such as of wind, thunder, or an explosion.

tweak and twack – *Tweak* means "to adjust or fine-tune." We're not sure what *twack* means, but it sounds a lot like Elmer Fudd saying "track."

VCR – Video Cassette Recorder.

visual effects – Things done during the shoot to create illusions, such as of leaves falling, wind, or snow. Explosions and car crashes, too, but don't go there.

wrap party – A little bash you throw after the shooting to say thank you to the cast and crew for all their hard work, and to try to buy their silence regarding the true story of what happened off-camera. Sometimes you serve wraps, or burritos, but usually not.

INDEX

Mark Shulman (co-author)

Mark Shulman writes for children and adults.

He was an early reader, an uncle at eight years old, a camp counselor, a radio newscaster, a New York City tour guide, and an advertising creative director before he started writing books. He is the youngest of five children, and he grew up with a Super 8 film camera. You got three minutes of film, couldn't erase any of it, had to mail your film to Kodak, send the equivalent of $30, and wait forever. After it came back, you had to edit with a razor blade and a bottle of glue, set up the noisy projector, turn out the lights, and then the projector light bulb would burn holes in your film. Mark loves video.

Mark graduated from East High School in Rochester, New York, and the University of Buffalo. He and his wife, Kara, live with little Hannah in New York, where she is videotaped mercilessly.

Hazlitt Krog (co-author)

Hazlitt Krog is a multimedia producer, creating videos, web sites, and music for love and/or money. His earliest memory is of playing with a Kodak Brownie camera under his crib. The youngest of four, he grew up an hour's drive due west of Mark.

Hazlitt got his first Super 8 movie camera, editing block, and projector at age 12 and was hooked. After graduating from Fredonia State University with a degree in Music, Video, and Film Production, his first job out of college was working on a Hollywood film called *The Natural*. He met Mark quite by accident on the phone. Soon after, they got together to make a boring training video about a humongous pump, and one of the early music videos. They've had many creative collaborations between that time and this book.

Hazlitt, his wife, Alexia, and their two Birman cats live on a hillside in Marin City, California, overlooking Mount Tam and the San Francisco Bay.

Martha Newbigging (illustrator)

Martha Newbigging was lucky enough to grow up with two art teachers as parents. She started making animated films and flip books at the age of nine. She and her brother often hosted basement screenings for the neighborhood kids, showing their own Super 8 cartoons along with films borrowed from the local library.

Martha graduated from the Ontario College of Art in Toronto. She continues to create animation using a combination of film, video, and computers. This is the fifth children's book she has illustrated and her animated films have been shown around the world.